D0819453

WE KNOW VAMPIRES, DULLAHANS, AND OTHER SO-CALLED "DEMI-HUMANS" FROM MYTH AND LEGEND.

THEY ARE NOT MERELY IMAGINARY, HOWEVER, BUT EXIST AMONG US AS MEMBERS OF SOCIETY.

POPULARLY KNOWN AS "DEMIS," DEMI-HUMANS ARE NOW RECOGNIZED AS PEOPLE...

...BUT THEY REMAIN SO RARE THAT IN THEIR ELUSIVENESS, AT LEAST, THEY ARE AKIN TO THEIR MYTHICAL BRETHREN.

—FROM NOTES ON DEMI-HUMANS

NOTES ON DEMI-HUMANS

YES...

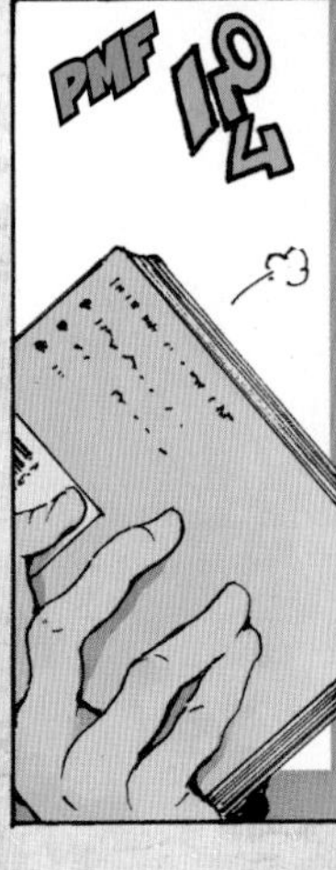

BUT MY SCHOOL SEEMS TO BE FULL OF THEM.

Characters

Vampire
Hikari Takanashi
1-B

- Likes liver, tomato juice.
- Receives blood from the government once a month.
- Opinions on romance: plenty; actual experience: none.

Dullahan
Kyoko Machi
1-B

- A demi from Irish folklore whose head and body are separate.
- Likes her head to be held.
- In love with Takahashi-sensei.

Snow Woman
Yuki Kusakabe
1-A

- Exudes cold air and weeps ice under stress.
- Avoids contact with others due to doubts about her own nature.

Succubus
Sakie Sato

- Math teacher.
- Lives in an isolated, dilapidated house so as not to unintentionally attract anyone.
- Romantic history: zilch.
- Has a crush on Takahashi-sensei.

Tetsuo Takahashi

- Biology teacher.
- Fascinated by demi studies since college.
- Tries his best to understand demis.

Himari Takanashi
1-C

- Hikari's younger twin sister. Human.
- Good grades, mature attitude—polar opposite of her sister.

 *DEMIS: SHORT FOR "DEMI-HUMANS." 

INTERVIEWS WITH MONSTER GIRLS

Volume 2

740.9999
I6126
v.2

INTERVIEWS WITH MONSTER GIRLS

CONTENTS

INTERVIEWS WITH MONSTER GIRLS

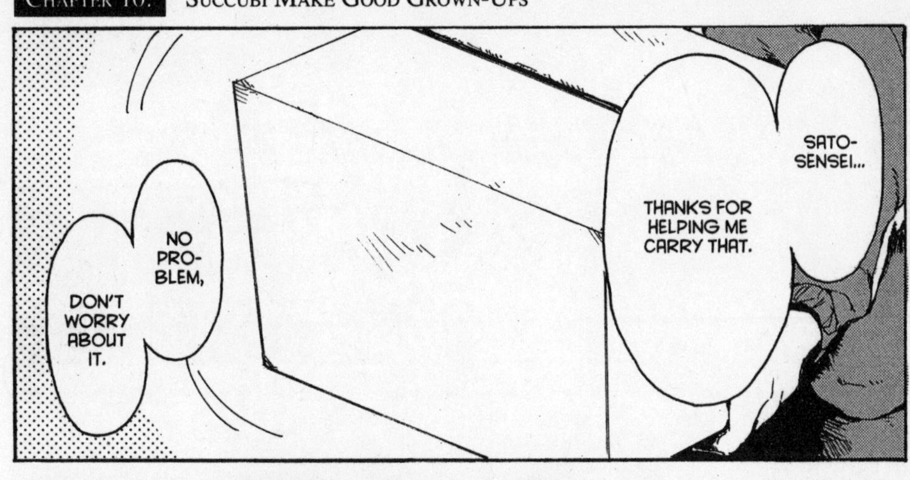

I KNOW YOUR HOMEROOM TEACHER CAN BE A LITTLE DENSE, MACHI-SAN.

ASKING A DULLAHAN TO CARRY A BOX ALL BY HERSELF!

HA HA...

SATO-SENSEI...

SHE'S SO PRETTY, AND NICE... SHE JUST SEEMS SO GROWN-UP...

I'M SURE SHE'S...

...BEEN IN LOVE...

...LOTS OF TIMES, TOO.

REFERENCE ROOM

IT LOOKS LIKE THIS BOOK BELONGS OVER THERE, TOO.
COULD YOU HANDLE IT?
S-SURE!

...

SATO-SENSEI...
HM?
ACTUALLY, I...WANTED TO TALK TO YOU...

I...
WELL...
THERE'S SOMEONE I LIKE...

OH, REALLY?
THAT'S GREAT!
ARE THEY A STUDENT AT OUR SCHOOL?

N-NO...
I MEAN...IT IS SOMEONE AT OUR SCHOOL, JUST NOT...
...?

I HAVE A...
I HAVE A CRUSH ON TAKAHASHI-SENSEI...

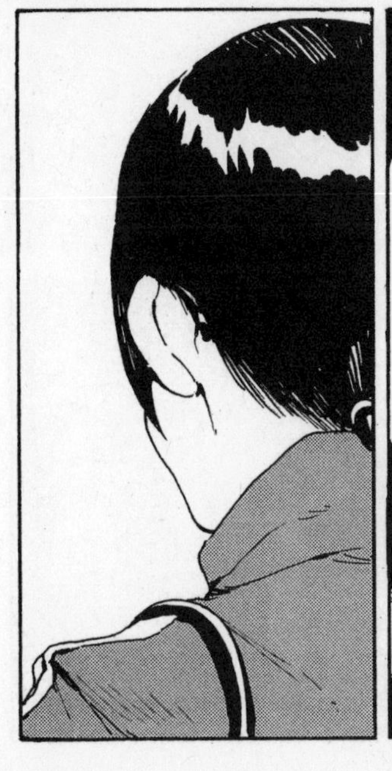

SO DO I.

...
WHAT AM I, STUPID?
...AS IF WE WERE RIVALS...
SHE'S A STUDENT! I'M A TEACHER!
...?

OH...OH, REALLY? COLOR ME SURPRISED...
S-SO, WHAT DID YOU WANT TO TALK TO ME ABOUT...?
OH,
WELL,
I WAS THINKING...

I-I WANT TO BE A GOOD MATCH FOR TAKAHASHI-SENSEI...
...BUT I'M AFRAID...
...MAYBE I'M JUST...
...TOO CHILDISH.

AND I WANT TO BE MORE GROWN-UP, BUT...
...I DON'T QUITE KNOW HOW TO DO THAT.

SO I WANTED TO TALK TO YOU...
WHY ME?

I-IT'S HARD TO EXPLAIN...
YOU'RE JUST...
IN MY MIND, YOU SEEM LIKE THE PICTURE OF A COOL GROWN-UP WOMAN...

A-AND YOU LOOK LIKE YOU'VE GOT *TONS* OF LOVE EXPERIENCE!
O-OH, DO I...?
APPEARANCES CAN BE DECEIVING...
XP: 0

...

YOU KNOW, MACHI-SAN...
BEING GROWN-UP...
...ISN'T REALLY ALL IT'S CRACKED UP TO BE.
VWSH
?

A GROWN-UP...
VWSH
...HUH?

TMP

SORRY IF IT SOUNDS LIKE I'M TALKING DOWN TO YOU...
THMP
!
...BUT WHAT LOOKS LIKE "BEING GROWN-UP" FROM A KID'S PERSPECTIVE...
...IS MOSTLY...
...A FACADE.
W-WHAT DO YOU MEAN...
...A FACADE?
JUST THAT.
YOU WANT TO MAKE A GOOD IMPRESSION ON EVERYONE...
OR YOU WANT KIDS TO RESPECT YOU...
...SO YOU PUT UP A FRONT.
I GUESS THAT MAKES ADULTS SOUND AWFULLY VAIN.
BUT PEOPLE IN MY LINE OF WORK, ESPECIALLY...
...JUST WANT TO LOOK GOOD.

YOU MEAN YOU'RE JUST PRETENDING, SATO-SENSEI?
HMM, I WONDER...
YES. 100%.
NO NEED TO ACT TOO SERIOUS WITH A STUDENT...

T-TAKAHASHI-SENSEI...
...TOO?

I WONDER...
TAKAHASHI-SENSEI AND I ARE BOTH "GROWN-UPS" IN THE STRICT SENSE...
ALTHOUGH OUR AGES ARE ABOUT AS FAR APART AS YOURS AND MINE.

BUT ONE THING I CAN TELL YOU...
...IS THAT EVEN TO ME, TAKAHASHI-SENSEI LOOKS...
...VERY GROWN-UP.

HE'S SO NATURAL.
SOMEHOW RELIABLE, EVEN WHEN HE'S JOKING AROUND.
HE'S FRIENDLY WITH EVERYONE...
...BUT NEVER PRIES SO MUCH HE HURTS ANYONE.
I THINK HE'S GREAT.
HE'S COOL...
HE'S...
STAAAA-AARE
A-ANYWAY, THE POINT IS—
IT'S HARD TO BE AN ADULT ON THE INSIDE...
...SO WHY NOT START WITH THE OUTSIDE?
YOU KNOW, FASHION! HAIRSTYLE!
R-RIGHT... THAT SOUNDS LIKE A GOOD IDEA...
...
BUT...
MY HAIR...
?

I CAN'T...
I CAN'T LET IT GROW LONG...
SLIP
BECAUSE IT GETS HARD TO HOLD...

OH,
OF COURSE!
I'M SORRY, I WASN'T THINKING...

I-IT'S OKAY.
I CAN'T GROW IT LONG, BUT I CAN STILL CHANGE THE STYLE.

B-BUT WHEN I ASKED TAKAHASHI-SENSEI ABOUT IT, HE SAID...
WOW, GREAT IDEA!
I SEE.
I'M GLAD YOU'RE A DULLAHAN, THOUGH, MACHI.

?

IT MEANS WE'VE GOT THE SAME HAIRSTYLE!
HA HA!
AND THAT JUST...
...MADE ME SO HAPPY.
SO I...
I THOUGHT MAYBE I'D JUST KEEP THIS STYLE FOREVER...
YOU KNOW?
...

YOU'RE SO LUCKYYYY!!

ばたばたばたばたばたばた

KICK KICK KICK KICK KICK

? ?

??

XP: 0

XP: 1

I-I'M JUST CURIOUS, MACHI-SAN... WHAT DREW YOU TO TAKAHASHI-SENSEI?
OH,
UM...

LIKE YOU SAID, SATO-SENSEI.
HOW HE'S...
...KIND...
...AND TRUST-WORTHY...
OH,
AND ...

HIS ARMS.
THEY'RE SO BUILT!

I KNOW !!

INTERVIEWS WITH MONSTER GIRLS

Chapter 11: Himari Takanashi's Trust Issues

HEY, I HEAR YOU DID GREAT ON YOUR RECENT TEST, HIMARI-CHAN.
DO YOU ALWAYS STUDY IN THE READING ROOM?
OH, UH, THANK YOU.
Y-YEAH. THEN I READ SOME BOOKS TO REFRESH MYSELF...
THE TRUTH IS...

...I DON'T TRUST TAKAHASHI-SENSEI.
NOT YET.

I APPRECIATE THAT HE'S KIND TO MY SISTER.
BUT SOMETIMES I WONDER.
...
IS IT JUST HIS INTEREST IN DEMIS?
DOES HE SEE HER AS A SUBJECT IN SOME EXPERIMENT?

OOPS! I FORGOT TO SET UP FOR TOMORROW'S EXPERIMENT!
EXPERIMENT?!

I HOPE THERE ARE ENOUGH MATERIALS FOR EVERY-ONE...
AHH, I'LL WORRY ABOUT IT TO-MORROW.
OH... HE MEANS FOR HIS CLASS...

AM I BEING TOO SENSITIVE?
I KNOW HE LIKES DEMIS, BUT...

NO WAY ANYONE IS JUST THINKING ABOUT VAMPIRES 24/7...
OH!
RIGHT!
I WANTED TO ASK YOU SOME QUESTIONS ABOUT VAMPIRES...
HE *WAS* THINKING ABOUT THEM?!
WHOA!

W-WELL... I'LL TELL HIM WHAT I CAN...
Y-YES?
WHAT DID YOU WANT TO KNOW...?

HA HA HA!
IT SEEMS LIKE HIKARI WOULD EAT GARLIC ALL DAY AND ALL NIGHT IF YOU LET HER.
WELL, ONE OF THE MOST WELL-KNOWN "FACTS" ABOUT VAMPIRES IS THAT THEY HATE GARLIC...
RIGHT ...
...AND I'VE BEEN THINKING, MAYBE THAT ISN'T QUITE RIGHT.

UH... HUH.
HE'S OB-SESSED!

MY CLUE WAS VAMPIRES' TENDENCY TO ATTACK PEOPLE WHO ARE LOST AT NIGHT.
WHY WOULD THEY ATTACK PEOPLE AT NIGHT?
HUH...

...BECAUSE THEY HATE SUNLIGHT?
TRUE, BUT THAT WOULD LEAVE THEM ABOUT EVEN WITH THEIR PREY.
THEY WOULDN'T BE SCARY ENOUGH TO WARRANT CARRYING CROSSES.

SOME OF THE LITERATURE SUGGEST VAMPIRES HAVE HEIGHTENED SENSES.
I THINK THAT'S THE REASON.

NIGHT LOOKS LIKE DAY TO THEM.
THEIR EARS CAN TRACK A PERSON.
THEIR NOSES PICK UP THE SCENT OF BLOOD.
MORE THAN ENOUGH TO STAY ONE STEP AHEAD OF A HUMAN IN THE DARK...

RIGHT.
THE POINT IS...
...THEIR EXCELLENT SENSE OF SMELL.
...!

THEIR EXCEPTIONAL NOSES CAUSE THEM TO DISLIKE FOODS WITH A STRONG ODOR.
I BELIEVE THAT'S THE SOURCE OF THE LEGEND THAT VAMPIRES HATE GARLIC!

AND WHAT DO SHARP SENSES HAVE TO DO...
...WITH GARLIC?

ANYWAY, THAT'S MY CONCLUSION.
WHAT DO YOU THINK?
DOES HIKARI SEEM TO HAVE EXCEPTIONAL SENSES?
...

SO WHY IS HIKARI SO KEEN ON GARLIC?
HER PALATE'S... A LITTLE TOO WIDE.

...YES.
I THINK YOU'RE EXACTLY RIGHT.
HER SENSES ARE GREAT.
OH!
COOL!

ONCE SHE WAS EATING SOMETHING REALLY SMELLY...
...AND I GOT WORRIED.
I WANTED TO MAKE SURE SHE WASN'T FORCING HERSELF TO EAT IT.
NO WORRIES!

I...
...LOVE THE STINKY STUFF!

Y-YOU WOULDN'T WANT TO ADVERTISE THAT...
FOR SURE...
HMMM...

...
YOU KNOW...
ON THAT NOTE...

A LOT OF PEOPLE TELL ME...
...HIKARI'S NOT VERY VAMPIRE-LIKE.
THAT SHE'S PRETTY MUCH LIKE A NORMAL SCHOOL-GIRL.

YOU SEEM VERY INTERESTED IN THE WAY DEMIS ARE, TAKAHASHI-SENSEI.
SO, WHAT DO YOU THINK?
IS MY SISTER REALLY MUCH OF A VAMPIRE?

OR ARE YOU NOT THAT INTEREST-ED...
...IN HER HUMANITY?

...

ガリガリ
SCRATCH SCRATCH
...
HUH.
GOOD QUES-TION.

IT'S TRUE HIKARI...

...DOESN'T BEHAVE THE WAY YOU'D EXPECT OF A VAMPIRE.

BUT DOES THAT MAKE HER "NOT VERY VAMPIRE-LIKE"?

I DON'T THINK SO.

!

...

HIKARI WANTS TO DRINK BLOOD FROM PEOPLE, BUT MAKES DO WITH THE BLOOD PACKS.

SHE HAS A VAMPIRE'S NOSE, BUT STILL ENJOYS STRONG-SMELLING FOOD.

THAT'S WHAT MAKES HER WHO SHE IS. SHE'S A VAMPIRE, YES, BUT ALSO A UNIQUE PERSON.
WE AREN'T BORN "LIKE" SOMETHING. WE TAKE WHAT WE'RE BORN WITH, AND LIVE OUR LIVES.

...
IF WE FOCUS ON "DEMI-HOOD," WE LOSE SIGHT OF THE INDIVIDUAL.
WE HAVE TO REMEMBER THAT EVERYONE IS DIFFERENT... BUT WE CAN'T TURN THAT INTO AN EXCUSE FOR NOT TRYING TO UNDERSTAND WHAT DEMIS ARE.
BECAUSE SO MANY OF DEMIS' PARTICULAR CONCERNS ARE BASED ON WHO AND WHAT THEY ARE.
THERE'S NEVER JUST ONE WAY OF SEEING THINGS.
WE NEED MORE PERSPEC-TIVES.

BUT IF WE SEE ONLY THEIR UNIQUENESS, WE WON'T REACH THE ROOTS OF THEIR WORRIES.
!!
GULP

BOTH ARE CRUCIAL.
...

AND WE HAVE TO STRIKE A BALANCE.

THAT'S WHAT I THINK, ANYWAY.

I'M STILL A BIT DOUBTFUL...
...BUT...
WHAT CAN I SAY?

MAYBE I REALLY CAN...
...COUNT ON HIM...

TAKAHASHI-SENSEI SEEMS LIKE...
...SOMEONE I CAN TRUST...
DING ♪
!

GOT A TEXT...
FROM SIS...
VWIP

SEN-SEI...
HUH?
I HAVE A QUES-TION...

JUST WHAT DID YOU HOPE TO LEARN ABOUT MY SISTER BY GIVING HER A HUG?

WAS IT ABOUT HER "VAMPIRE NATURE"?

GOT A HUG FROM SENSEI TODAY! HE TOTALLY JUMPED ME!

OR ABOUT HER "INDIVIDUAL NATURE"?

"GOT A HUG"?!
"JUMPED ME"?!
WHAT IN THE WORLD IS SHE SAYING?!
D-DON'T MISUNDERSTAND, HIMARI!
SHE WAS THE ONE WHO-
...
YOU CRACKPOT, DEMI-LOVING TEACHER!!
GAAAAH!!
WELL, YOU'RE NOT WRONG, BUT-!

LATER, SHE GOT THE TRUTH.
SO?
WHY SEND A TEXT I WOULD TAKE THE WRONG WAY?
SORRY ...
SIGH

YOU'VE BEEN OUT SO LATE THESE DAYS, HIMARI.
I WAS BORED HERE...
I THOUGHT THAT TEXT MIGHT...
...GET YOU HOME QUICKER.
WHO KNEW YOU WERE WITH HIM RIGHT THEN?

...

YOU COULD JUST TEXT ME "COME HOME SOON." I'LL LISTEN, YOU KNOW.
YOU WILL?!
YOU'RE THE BEST, HIMARI!

INTERVIEWS WITH MONSTER GIRLS

I DECIDED TO HIDE THAT I WAS A SNOW WOMAN WHEN I GOT TO HIGH SCHOOL.
MAYBE THEN PEOPLE WOULDN'T COME UP TO ME JUST TO SEE A DEMI UP CLOSE.
MAYBE NO ONE WOULD GET HURT BECAUSE OF WHAT I WAS.
BUT THEN, ONE DAY IN APRIL...
...THE HEAT GOT THE BETTER OF ME DURING GYM...
Y-YOU ALL RIGHT, KUSAKABE?
ERK
HE WAS GOING TO TOUCH ME, AND I JUST BLURTED IT OUT–

Chapter 12: Snow Women Are Cold (Part 1)

I'M...
...A SNOW WOMAN...
IF I...
...COOL DOWN, I'LL BE FINE.
LATER, I COLLAPSED.
...!!
...
...
THEY CARRIED ME ON A STRETCHER...
...!!

...

...
...

DID YOU...
...ALWAYS HIDE...
!

...THE FACT YOU'RE A SNOW WOMAN?
EVEN BEFORE HIGH SCHOOL?

N-NO!
I NEVER HID IT BEFORE...
AT ALL...

UNTIL HIGH SCHOOL, I LIVED IN A RURAL AREA THAT GOT A LOT OF SNOW.
I NEVER QUESTIONED WHAT IT MEANT TO BE A SNOW WOMAN.
I HAD A BELOW-AVERAGE BODY TEMPER-ATURE...
...AND SOMETIMES MY BREATH FOGGED OR I CRIED ICE CRYSTALS...
...
SO...
...AFTER YOU MOVED HERE, BUT BEFORE YOU STARTED HIGH SCHOOL...
...
...SOME-THING...
...HAPP-ENED.
...BUT THAT WAS IT. IT DIDN'T AFFECT ANYONE ELSE.
...
Y-
YES.
SOME-THING...
LIKE...
THAT.

IT WAS...
...JUST AFTER I MOVED HERE.
I WAS SO DEPRESSED.
NORMALLY I DON'T DO MUCH THINKING IN THE TUB.
BUT LIFE IN A NEW PLACE HAD ME VERY WORRIED...
I'D LEFT BEHIND FRIENDS I'D KNOWN ALL THE WAY THROUGH MIDDLE SCHOOL...
I WASN'T SURE I COULD MAKE IT WORK.
I'D NEVER LIVED IN A BIG CITY, AND IT SCARED ME...
IT WOULD BE SO MUCH EASIER IF I COULD MELT INTO THE WATER, LIKE IN THE STORIES...

RIGHT THEN, I NOTICED SOMETHING STRANGE.
?
HUH...?

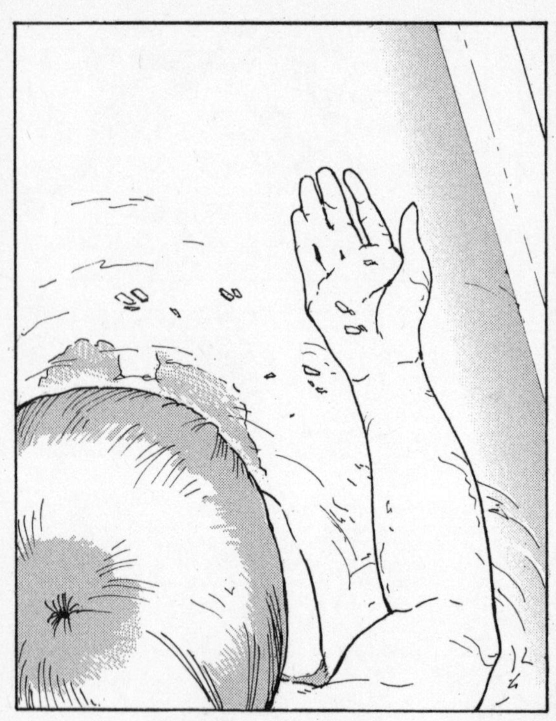

ICE...
...IN THE BATHTUB?

I WAS SHOCKED.
THE ICE MELTED RIGHT AWAY...
...BUT I REALIZED I COULD FREEZE A HOT BATH WITH MY CHILL.
AND THAT WAS TERRIFYING.

GRAAAAHH!!
WHAT IF THAT ABILITY WERE TURNED...
HI-YAH!
...ON A HUMAN BEING?
THAT'S ...
...WHAT WAS ON MY MIND...
...AS I STARTED HIGH SCHOOL.
I THOUGHT, MAYBE IF I DON'T TOUCH ANYONE, IT'LL BE ALL RIGHT...
SO I OPENLY AVOIDED PEOPLE.
BUT...
...
I...
I'M SCARED! I DON'T KNOW HOW DANGEROUS I REALLY AM...
IF I DID, I COULD LET PEOPLE KNOW.
AND THEN I COULD BE PROUD TO TELL THEM, "I'M A SNOW WOMAN"...
...
BE PROUD...
SHE'S A SNOW WOMAN...

NOTE: 40 DEGREES CELSIUS = 104 DEGREES FAHRENHEIT.

COULD SHE HAVE WEPT ICE TEARS INTO THE WATER?
HRRRRM...
NO...
IF SHE'D BEEN CRYING THEN, SHE WOULD'VE SUGGESTED THE POSSIBILITY HERSELF.

WHAT ELSE MIGHT FREEZE...?
SWEAT.
WERE YOU SWEATING?
MAYBE THAT FROZE IN THE WATER.
SWEAT...?

WELL...
ACTUALLY ...
...I DON'T SWEAT VERY MUCH.

REALLY ?

YES. HARDLY AT ALL, IN FACT.
I SWEAT LESS THAN OTHER PEOPLE, AND MY...
MY, UM... SWEAT GLANDS, IS THAT WHAT THEY'RE CALLED?
YEAH... THE VESSELS THAT PRODUCE SWEAT.
YES...
I HAVE VERY FEW OF THEM.

SWEAT GLANDS...

PEOPLE WHO LIVE IN TROPICAL PLACES ARE SAID TO HAVE MORE SWEAT GLANDS THAN THOSE WHO LIVE IN THE ARCTIC CIRCLE.

MORE SWEAT GLANDS MEANS BETTER BODY TEMPERATURE REGULATION.

SO A SNOW WOMAN WITHOUT MANY SWEAT GLANDS ***WOULD*** TAKE HEAT POORLY.

BUT DO YOU SWEAT ***SOME***, RIGHT?

COULD IT HAVE FROZEN?

IT'S TRUE...
I DO SWEAT A LITTLE.
BUT IT'S NEVER FROZEN BEFORE.
WHEN I CRY, MY TEARS ARE ALWAYS ICE...
WHY JUST THAT ONE TIME?

GOOD POINT...
HER TEARS ARE ALWAYS ICE?
HM...
THAT CAN'T BE EASY.

BOOK: *SNOW WOMEN*

THIS IS MY COLLECTED RESEARCH ON SNOW WOMEN LEGENDS.
I'VE BEEN COLLECTING THEM FROM BOOKS AND WEB SITES AND THE LIKE.
THEY ALL TELL ROUGHLY THE SAME STORY...
SHE'S A BEAUTIFUL WOMAN IN WHITE WITH LONG HAIR.
THOUGH SOMETIMES SHE'S AN OLD WOMAN...
AND THE PLOTS FOLLOW SIMILAR ARCS.
USUALLY, THE SNOW WOMAN APPROACHES A MAN WITHOUT REVEALING WHAT SHE IS.
THEN, (1) THE MAN REFUSES A REQUEST OF HERS, SO SHE DOES SOMETHING AWFUL TO HIM...
POW
1.
...OR (2) SHE BECOMES CLOSE TO HIM, BUT SOME ACCIDENT DRIVES HER TO VANISH.
2.
THERE ARE REGIONAL DISAGREEMENTS ABOUT WHETHER SHE'S A GHOST OR A FAIRY...
...BUT THEY'RE MINOR.
IT'S STRANGE. THE ONE THING THE STORIES HAVE IN COMMON...
...IS THAT THEY'RE ALWAYS TRAGIC.
...
OH
SOR...

!!!

DO YOUR FEET GET COLD WHEN YOU'RE NERVOUS...?
Y-YES, THEY DO...
MAYBE I GET COLD EASILY...?

...
...
KUSA-KABE...

I...
SEE...

CLATTER

RATTLE

...

HUH?

デュラハンちゃんは眠りたい
Goodnight Dullahan
Z
z
z

Goodnight Dullahan

Kyoko Machi
Class 1-B
Dullahan

·A demi from Irish myth, whose head and body are separate.
·Likes her head to be held.
·In love with Takahashi-sensei!

YURIKO... YOU AND I WERE MEANT TO...
NO, TAKKUN! WE CAN'T!

KYOKO-CHAAAAN!
WOULD YOU CHECK THE BATH WATER, PLEASE?
!
SURE THING!

HER BODY CAN GET AROUND BY ITSELF IN HER HOUSE.

AHHHH...
THAT FEELS GREAT...

IN THE BATH
MMMM!

SCRUB
SCRUB
SCRUB

ANY TICKLISH SPOTS, MA'AM?
OH HO HO...
JUST KIDDING.

TOWEL
PILLOW
SMALL DOG HOUSE FOR BED

...
WHAT A NICE DAY... I'LL JUST DRIFT OFF...

G'NIGHT...
FOOO...

CLASSES HAVE ONLY...
...GOTTEN TOUGHER IN HIGH SCHOOL...
GOTTA...
STUDY ...

...
GOTTA ...
STUDY ...
REVIEW ...
AND EXERCISE ...
...
I MIGHT BE...
IN...
...OVER MY HEAD...

ぱちっ
BLINK
がばぁ!!
WHUMPH!

FOOOO...
PHONE
TAP TAP

NEW MEMO (1)
I'M IN OVER
MY HEAD
USE WHEN
VERY BUSY
TAP...

IF YOU WANT YOUR FRIENDS TO BE WILLING TO HAVE A LITTLE FUN...
...YOU CAN SHOW WHAT IS AND ISN'T OKAY TO JOKE ABOUT...

...

SENSEI ...
WOULD YOU LAUGH AT THIS JOKE...?
SHE WAS LOOKING FORWARD TO THE WEEK AHEAD.

SEVERAL MINUTES LATER—TAKAHASHI-SENSEI HAS FILLED THE BASIN WITH HOT WATER.

SENSEI?

WHAT'S THAT...?

HOT WATER?

HUP.

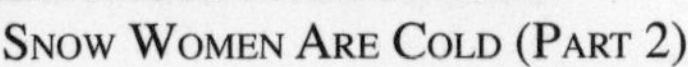

Chapter 13: Snow Women Are Cold (Part 2)

HOW'S THE TEMPER-ATURE?
FINE...
チャポン...
SPLISH...

UM...
WHY ARE WE...?
NOW,
HERE.
RUSTLE

COULD YOU...
...READ THIS ALOUD FOR ME?
VWIP
R-READ IT...?

FROM EARLIER...
THESE ARE YOUR NOTES...
...ON SNOW WOMAN STORIES...

THE ONE THING THE STORIES HAVE IN COMMON...
...IS THAT THEY'RE ALWAYS TRAGIC.
IS THIS...
...REALLY NECESS-ARY?

YES.
IT'S IMPOR-TANT.
I KNOW IT MUST BE VERY PAINFUL FOR YOU...
...
...BUT I WANT YOU TO REALLY THINK ABOUT THEM WHILE YOU READ...

...
ALL RIGHT.
AHEM...

"A SNOW WOMAN STORY FROM NIIGATA PRE-FECTURE."
"ONE WINTER NIGHT, IN A TERRIBLE BLIZZARD, A PALE, BEAUTIFUL WOMAN WITH LONG HAIR CAME TO A MAN..."
...
"HER BODY WAS COLD AS ICE, SO HE URGED HER TO TAKE A BATH, BUT SHE ADAMANTLY REFUSED."
"WHEN HE FORCED HER INTO THE BATH WATER, SHE MELTED AWAY... ONLY A BIT OF AN ICICLE REMAINED..."
...GO ON.
...OKAY.
...
THIS IS VERY PAINFUL FOR KUSAKABE.
I HATE TO HURT HER LIKE THIS.
BUT IF MY GUESS IS CORRECT...
ぴゃ...
BRRR...
!

SHE'S GIVING OFF A CHILL...
BUT NOT ENOUGH TO FREEZE WATER...

"SHE ..."
"AND ..."
"IN RESPONSE ..."

"A CHILDREN'S FABLE."
"THERE ONCE WAS A VILLAGE WHERE TWO WOODCUTTERS LIVED."
"ONE DAY, CAUGHT IN A BLIZZARD..."
"...THEY SOUGHT SHELTER IN A SMALL HUT."
"ALONG CAME A WOMAN DRESSED IN WHITE, WITH COLD EYES..."

"SHE BREATHED UPON THE TWO SLEEPING MEN..."
"...AND TURNED THEM... TO ICE..."
...

...
MAYBE I HAVE NO RIGHT TO MAKE HER DO THIS...
...BUT I WANT TO HELP HER.
IT WILL GO WELL. IT WILL GET BETTER.

IF SHE CAN JUST GET THROUGH THIS, I'M SURE...
"THOUGH ..."
"THE MEN ..."
"...DID NOT DIE..."

THE WATER...?

...!!

KUSA-KABE!
YES?
THE WATER—!

FLOAT...
プカ…

WHA?!
I-ICE?!
YEEK!
ギャッ

...

WHA...
WHAT ...?
...

...
STAAAARE
じぃ…
...

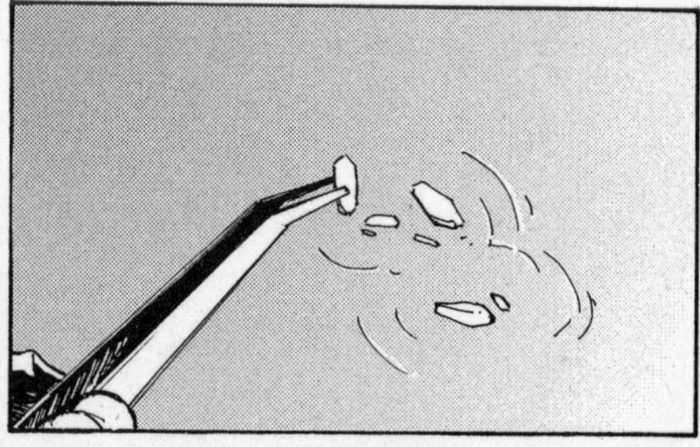

YEP.
IT IS ICE.
I KNEW IT.
YOU DID?

YES...
KUSA-KABE.
THIS ICE IS SWEAT.
THE SWEAT FROM YOUR FEET...
...JUST FROZE.

THIS IS THE PRODUCT OF MENTAL STRESS.

YOU'VE HEARD OF *BREAKING OUT IN A COLD SWEAT?*

A...

A COLD SWEAT ...?

IS THAT REAL?

THAT'S JUST A *MANGA THING...*

...ISN'T IT?

I SEE.

YOU DIDN'T KNOW ABOUT IT.

WE REALLY DO GET "COLD SWEATS."
IT'S MOST COMMON ON...
THE FORE-HEAD...
THE PALMS...
...AND THE SOLES OF THE FEET.
EVERYONE'S DIFFERENT, OF COURSE.
FOR EXAMPLE, MY FOREHEAD STAYS DRY, BUT MY PALMS TEND TO SWEAT EASILY.

KUSA-KABE...
IF YOUR FOREHEAD OR PALMS SWEATED MUCH...
...YOU WOULD'VE NOTICED.
BUT...
~~FOREHEAD~~
~~PALMS~~
SOLES
OH...

RIGHT. YOU GET "COLD SWEAT" ON THE BOTTOMS OF YOUR FEET.
FEW PEOPLE REALIZE, BUT THE SOLES OF THE FEET HAVE MORE SWEAT GLANDS THAN ALMOST ANYWHERE ELSE ON THE BODY.

...!!
DO YOUR FEET GET COLD WHEN YOU'RE NERVOUS...?
YES, THEY DO... MAYBE I GET COLD EASILY...?

...
するする...
TUG TUG

...THAT'S AMAZING.
BUT WHAT...
...MADE YOU THINK COLD SWEAT WOULD FREEZE?
AH...

THE CLUE...
...WAS IN THE STORIES.

THE STORIES ...?

NOT ALL TALES OF DEMIS ARE CHEERFUL...

...BUT SNOW WOMAN STORIES ARE ESPECIALLY RIFE WITH GRIEF.

UNREQUITED LOVE, SOCIAL ISOLATION, MELTING AWAY... EVERY LEGEND ENDS POORLY FOR THE SNOW WOMAN.

I REALIZED...

TO BE A SNOW WOMAN IS TO BE CONNECTED TO NEGATIVE EMOTIONS AND MENTAL BURDENS...

SO MAYBE STRESS-INDUCED SWEAT...
...
...WOULD FREEZE, TOO.
I'M SORRY FOR PUTTING YOU THROUGH THIS.
HUH?
TO RECREATE WHAT HAPPENED TO YOU IN THE BATH...
...I NEEDED YOU TO BE ANXIOUS.

YOU DON'T NEED TO WORRY ABOUT THE CHILL THAT EMANATES FROM YOUR BODY, EITHER.

IT'S BARELY ENOUGH TO COOL THE WATER.

YOU WERE RIGHT WHEN YOU SAID IT WOULDN'T AFFECT ANYONE ELSE.

YOU HAVE NOTHING TO WORRY ABOUT...

...

KUSA-KABE.

YOU'RE NOT...
...THE TYPE OF DEMI...
...WHO'D EVER HURT ANYONE.

...

...

THANK GOODNESS...

I'M SO...
...SO GLAD...

...
OF COURSE...

SNOW WOMEN ARE SHAPED BY NEGATIVE EMOTIONS...
...SO ONLY TEARS OF SADNESS FREEZE.

HAPPINESS...
...RELIEF...

THOSE WARM TEARS...

...DON'T FREEZE.

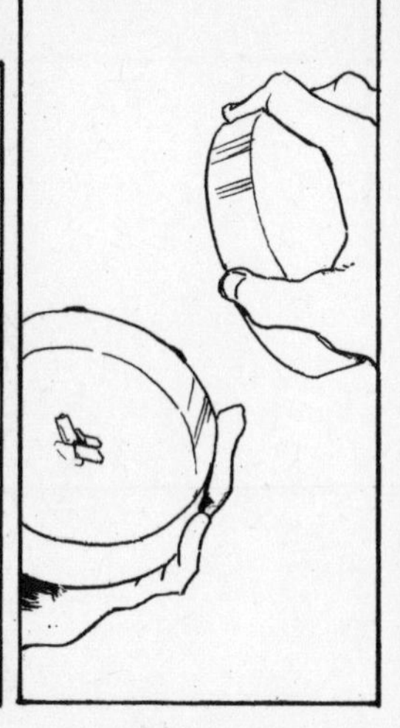

SQUEAK!
RUB ぐじ
!
RUB ぐじ

...

THAT ICE SWEAT...
WHAT WILL YOU DO WITH IT?
HUH?
WELL, SINCE IT'S HERE, I THOUGHT MAYBE I'D DO A COMPONENT ANALYSIS AT THE UNIVERSITY...
IT'S OUR ONE CHANCE.
WHA—?!
C— COMPONENT ANALYSIS?!

P- PLEASE DON'T!
GRAB ばっ
ISN'T THAT SEXUAL HARASS- MENT?!
AWWWW, REALLY?
A-A-A- ABSO- LUTELY NOT!
WHY NOT? YOU'RE SO COLD...
...

DUH!
I'M A SNOW WOMAN!

HOW WOULD YOU DESCRIBE WHAT'S HAPPENING HERE?
HMM...
THIS IS THE CRYSTAL-LIZATION OF BODILY FLUIDS PRODUCED UNDER STRESS...

IN A WORD—
—THE PRODUCT OF YOUR SWEAT AND TEARS!

SORRY, I'M... NOT SURE HOW TO REACT...
NO, MY FAULT... SORRY...
BAD JOKE...

INTERVIEWS WITH MONSTER GIRLS

Chapter 14: Demis, Buddies

HELLO! MACHI HERE!
CLASS IS OVER FOR TODAY AND I'M AT THE PARK...
I LOVE VANILLA!
...HAVING ICE CREAM WITH HIKARI-CHAN AND KUSAKABE-SAN!

BELIEVE IT OR NOT, KUSAKABE-SAN INVITED US!
I HAVEN'T TALKED MUCH WITH HER YET...

もひ
MUNCH
もひ
MUNCH

...SO I HOPE NOW...
...WE CAN BECOME BETTER FRIENDS!

MACCHII, YOU ALL RIGHT?
NO TROUBLE EATING?
N-NOPE!
I GOT IT IN A CUP, SO...
THANKS!

...

TAKA-NASHI-SAN...
WANT TO TRY A BITE OF MINE?
IT'S CHOCO-MINT.
HUH?
REALLY?
OKAY...

H-HERE YOU GO...
Y-YAAAY...

OH!

TOO CLOSE!
TOO CLOSE!

JOLT
WHOA!

...

H-HAND IT THIS WAY...
S-SURE...

THE MINT'S REFRESHING... YUM!
S-SURE IS...

...
WHEN YUKKII AND I FIRST MET...

...I USED TO GIVE HER...
...LOTS OF HUGS AND STUFF.

YUKKII MAY BE...
...A DEMI, TOO, BUT...
PLUS THERE WAS...
...THAT DAY...

BUT SHE DIDN'T SEEM TO LIKE IT MUCH...
...SO I'M TRYING TO KEEP MY DISTANCE.

I'M REALLY HAPPY YUKKII INVITED US OUT TODAY...
CRUNCH
...BUT SOMEHOW, I CAN'T QUITE SHOW IT...

!

WHAT DOES SHE THINK OF ME?
FIDGET FIDGET
カリカリ
HOW DOES YUKKII... FEEL ABOUT ME?

ちまっ
TINY

I'M SORRY, YUKKI!
I ALMOST FINISHED IT!
I-IT'S ALL RIGHT! DON'T WORRY!

...
カリ
カリ
FIDGET FIDGET

...

T-TAKA-NASHI-SAN...
AHEM...
?

I...
I WANTED TO APOLOGIZE TO YOU...
HUH?
...

A...
APOLO-GIZE?

T-TAKA-NASHI-SAN...
YOU KNEW I WAS TRYING TO AVOID PEOPLE...
...DIDN'T YOU?
!!
ERK...

SO...
YOU STOPPED GIVING ME HUGS...
...AND KEPT YOUR DISTANCE...
...

I WAS SO HAPPY AT HOW THOUGHTFUL YOU WERE...
BUT... IF...
IF I CAUSED YOU ANY UNHAPPI-NESS...
I'M REALLY... REALLY SORRY...
!

チラ…
GLANCE

…
うずうず
FIDGET FIDGET

SORRY, YUKKII, BUT...
...COULD I NIBBLE YOU? JUST A LITTLE?
?!
HUH?!
Y-YOU MEAN DRINK MY BLOOD?!
N-NO!

HOW DO I PUT THIS? I HAVE PLENTY OF BLOOD, BUT...
...SOMETIMES YOUR TEETH KIND OF ITCH, YOU JUST WANT TO BITE SOMETHING...
...BE A LITTLE ROUGH...
R-ROUGH...?

J-JUST LIGHTLY... OVER YOUR CLOTHES.
R-RIGHT...
I GUESS IT'S OKAY?
!!
REALLY ?!

OKAY, HERE GOES!
?!!
HYA-AH!
CHOMP

HYA-AH HA HA!
IT TICKLES...
NIBBLE
NIBBLE
NIBBLE
NIBBLE NIBBLE
HYAAA HA HA HA!
ST-
STOP!
NIBBLE NIBBLE

T-TAKANASHI-SAN, T... TIME OUT!
!

...

MACHI-SAN?

—

MACHI-SAN...

SO THERE ARE FEW HAPPY TALES OF DEMIS.

SNOW-WOMAN STORIES, ESPECIALLY...

...WERE, LIKE THE WOMEN THEMSELVES, OFTEN SAD.

BUT ARE MODERN-DAY SNOW WOMEN...

...CONSTRAINED TO WALK THE SAME PATH AS THEIR LEGENDARY FOREBEARS?

HARDLY.

WHY NOT?

SHEESH!

YOU GUYS ARE TOO MUCH!

HA HA HA HA!

BECAUSE THEY'RE WRITING A NEW STORY, IN WHICH SNOW WOMEN, DULLAHANS, AND VAMPIRES...

...ARE ALL BUDDIES TOGETHER.

WHAT DO YOU USUALLY DO WHEN YOU WANT TO BITE SOMEONE?
OH.
I ASK HIMARI.

HIMARI.
NIBBLES?
NIBBLES?
HER WORD SINCE CHILDHOOD

MM.

NIBBLE
NIBBLE
NEXT PAGE.
MM!
FLIP

INTERVIEWS WITH MONSTER GIRLS

OH HO.

GAB

GAB

OH!

MORNIN', SENSEI!

GAB

GOOD MORNING!

GOOD MORNING.

MORNING.

GLAD TO SEE YOU ALL SO FRIENDLY.

GAB

WELL,

Y' KNOW!

YEP!

THAT'S RIGHT!

HIKARI AND KYOKO TREAT ME SO WELL!

...

HIKARI!
YOU BETTER WATCH OUT...
AWWW, WHY ME?
THAT HURTS!
CAUSE A SCENE, YOU'LL GET IN TROUBLE!
...
WHY DO YOU CALL *HER* HIKARI?
TAKAHASHI-SENSEI...
UM...

O-OH!
TO DISTINGUISH HER FROM HIMARI-CHAN...
TAKANASHI
HIKARI HIMARI
OH, HIMARI-CHAN, IS IT?
UMMM...

...
...

...
...

??
?
?
?

...
AHEM...
UM...

MORNING, TAKANASHI.
G-GOOD MORNING... SENSEI...?
IS THIS A LECTURE?
IT FEELS AWKWARD TO START NOW...

HIKARI-
CHAAAN!
RIGHT 'ERE!
OBNOXIOUS REACTION.

HIKARI.
HUH? WHAT?

...
I...
I GUESS I GET IT...

IN THAT CASE...
...
WHY NOT CALL KYOKO BY HER NAME, TOO?
!

HUH? I DON'T MIND EITHER WAY.
HOW ABOUT YOU?
KYOKO ?

WHA-WHUMPH!

...

OH...
...“MACHI” IS FINE.
YOU KNOW...
?
...
OKAY...

"MACHI" KIND OF SOUNDS LIKE A FIRST NAME, TOO...
...AND I LIKE BEING CALLED THAT.

ARE YOU SURE,
KYOKO?
Y-
YEAH.
YUKI-CHAN...
IT'S KIND OF EMBAR-RASSING.
AND...

...
OKAY.

OKAY!
RIGHT!

DELIBERATIONS ABOUT WHAT TO CALL EACH OTHER OUGHT TO START WITH THIS GIRL...
AW-WW!
HE GOT ME!

YOU'RE FULL OF *YUKKIIS* AND *MACCHIIS!*
BUT I'M JUST "SENSEI"? WHY NOT "TAKAHASHI-SENSEI," OR "TETSU-SENSEI"?
WHAT HAPPENED TO "TETSUO TAKAHASHI"?
AWW, WELL...

SENSEI, YOU JUST...
...SORTA SEEM LIKE A SENSEIII!
WHAT ARE YOU TALKING ABOUT?!
SHE'S RIGHT.
TOTALLY!

BUT IT'S NOT UNUSUAL TO CALL A TEACHER "SENSEI," IS IT?
NO.
BUT SHE ADDRESSES ALL THE OTHER TEACHERS BY NAME.
HIKARI.
KATO, THE JAPANESE TEACHER, IS...?
KATO-SENSEI.
AND YACHIGUSA, THE NURSE?
YACHIGUSA-SENSEI.
SEE?

!
COME TO THINK OF IT, WHAT DO YOU CALL SATO-SENSEI?
HM?

"SAKKII"!
SAKKII??!!
WHAT ARE YOU, FRIENDS?!
HA HA HA!

YEESH.
SO MUCH DRAMA. THEY'RE JUST NAMES...
...
REALLY...

OKAY, I'D BETTER...
OH...

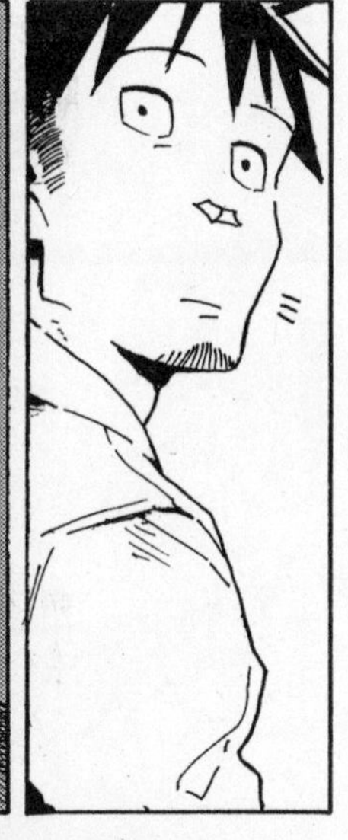

SOME-THING WRONG?
...
...NO.
UM...
AHEM...

IT'S...
...NO-THING.
NEVER-MIND...

TAP
...
UH... SURE...

CATCH YOU LATER, THEN...

YUKI.
!!
FWAH
...
...
HA HA...
I JUST THOUGHT MAYBE YOU'D WANT TO BE CALLED THAT.
A HUNCH.

IT DOESN'T MATTER THAT MUCH WHAT WE CALL EACH OTHER, RIGHT?

HUH?

YOU BROUGHT IT UP...

INTERVIEWS WITH MONSTER GIRLS

INTERVIEWS WITH MONSTER GIRLS

Chapter 16: A Boy Called Kurtz

...

ぐずっ
SNIFF...

HE'S SO PRETTY!

I'M SAKIE SATO.
I TEACH MATH.
HOW ABOUT YOU?
SAKIE-SENSEI...!
I...
I'M KURTZ.
NICE TO MEET YOU.
KURTZ YOUNG BOY
KURTZ...
DO YOU HAVE GERMAN ANCESTRY, BY ANY CHANCE?
Y-YES, I DO! I'M IMPRESSED YOU KNOW THAT!
O-OH, HARDLY!
I HAPPENED TO STUDY GERMAN IN COLLEGE...
SO...

...WHAT ARE YOU DOING HERE, KURTZ-KUN?
!

OH, UH...
SOMEONE WAS WITH ME...
...BUT WE GOT SEPARATED.

SO THAT'S WHY HE WAS CRYING BY HIMSELF.
DID A PARENT BRING YOU?
WILL YOU BE TRANS-FERRING HERE?
OH...
UH-HH...

YEAH...
GRIN
APPARENTLY NOT...

I FEEL BAD LYING TO A NICE PERSON LIKE SAKIE-SENSEI...BUT THERE'S NO CHOICE!
I CAN'T LET HER KNOW WHAT I REALLY AM!
I HAVE TO CONVINCE HER I'M A TRANSFER STUDENT, LOOKING FOR MY FATHER!
NOTE: ALREADY FOUND OUT

HE'S CLEARLY LYING ABOUT BEING A TRANSFER...
SHOULD I PRESS HIM?
HE DOESN'T SEEM LIKE A BAD KID, THOUGH... HMM...

GAB GAB
!
OH!
HI, SATO-SENSEI!
HI, SATO-SENSEI!
HELLO, GIRLS...
...

FOOOO
HER HEAD...
YES.
SHE'S A DEMI-HUMAN—A DULLAHAN.
REALLY? SHE IS?
OH!
INTERESTED IN DEMI-HUMANS, KURTZ-KUN?
NOT REALLY...
YOU TOTALLY ARE.

THAT WAS CLOSE.
MY TRUE SELF...
...AND MY GOAL...
...MUST NOT BE SUS-PECTED!
NOTE: ALREADY SUS-PECTED

...
...

HE'S INTERESTED IN DEMI-HUMANS... I SHOULD TRY TO TALK WITH HIM.
BUT I DON'T THINK HE'D BE HONEST WITH ME...

I COULD ATTRACT HIM AND THEN MAKE HIM TELL ME...!
NO, NO, NO, NO, NO!
WHY DO I THINK THESE THINGS? ARGH!
スッ
VWIP

UM, WHERE ARE YOU–?
LET'S GO FIND YOUR PARENT.
THAT SEEMS LIKE THE QUICKEST SOLUTION.
KRACK

COME ON!
LOS GEHTS!
OH...
W...

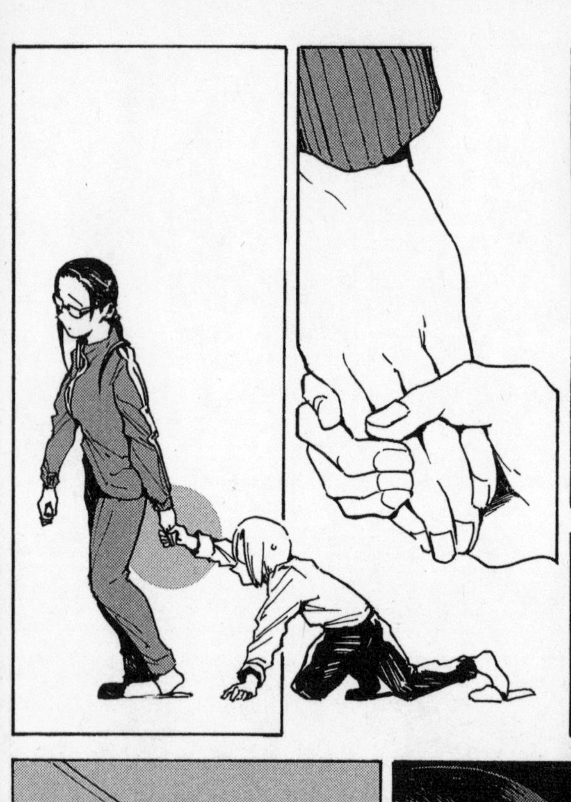

JERK
WAI...
?!

OH NO...

?
HUH?

HE'S...NOT ATTRACTED...?

I KNOW PEOPLE WITH EXTREMELY LOW LIBIDOS SOMETIMES AREN'T, BUT...
...
...
BUT I WOULDN'T TAKE HIM FOR THE TYPE.

THERE'S SOMETHING...
?
...MORE TO THIS BOY...
DOES SHE SUSPECT...?
KA-THUMP
KA-THUMP

SATO-SEN-SEI!
!

TAKAHASHI-SENSEI!

IS SOMETHING WRONG?

Y- YEAH ...

HIKARI SAID SHE SAW AN INTRUDER ON CAMPUS...
A-AN INTRUDER?!

WE'RE TALKING ABOUT HIKARI, SO SHE MIGHT HAVE EMBELLISHED A BIT.
...
ANYWAY, BE CAREFUL.
AN INTRUDER...

SOMEONE WAS WITH ME...
...BUT WE GOT SEPARATED.
...

...
MAYBE ...
...

SAKIE-SENSEI LOOKS SO SERIOUS... SHE'S REALLY WORRIED ABOUT THIS INTRUDER...
NOTE: WRONG

SHE MAY SUSPECT ME...
...AND I'VE GOT TO KEEP HER TRUST.

NO...I'VE GOT TO REPAY HER KINDNESS.
WHOEVER IT IS...
I'LL DEAL WITH THEM.

WHO'S HE?
ABOUT THAT...

HIS NAME IS KURTZ-KUN. HE GOT SEPARATED FROM WHO-EVER HE WAS WITH.
I'M WONDERING IF THAT PERSON IS OUR "INTRUDER."
I'LL TAKE YA!
I SEE...

CLACK
CLACK
CLACK

HEY, HIKARI SAID THE INTRUDER WAS "A GUY AS BIG AS A BEAR."
OH YEAH?
KINDA LIKE YOU?
HEH.
CLACK
CLACK
BUH?
HUH?
CLACK
CLACK
!

OH, I'M SURE HE'S MUCH TALLER THAN M—

SHOOP

ぬ

WHACK
?!!
GRAB
HRR
HWAH!

SLAM

EEYOW!

YEEK!
YIPES!

ARE YOU OKAY, SAKIE-SENSEI?!
OW OW OW OW OWW
ギギギギ
PULL PULL PULL PULL
UH, YEAH...
THAT WAS REALLY SOME-THING.
...

U...
UGAKI-SAN?

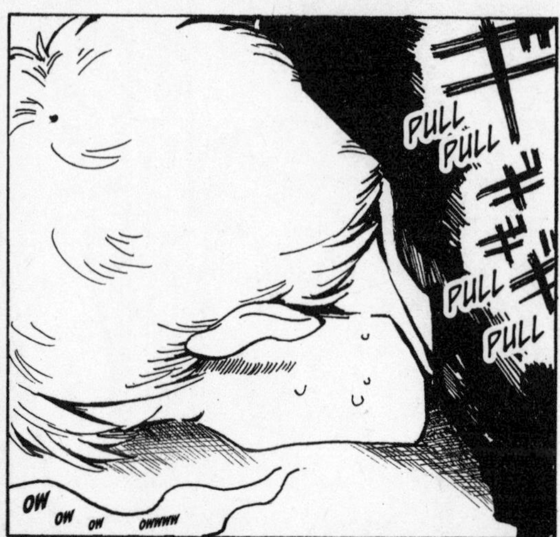
PULL PULL
PULL PULL
OW OW OW OWWWW

UGAKI-SAN...?

SWEAAAAAT

UGAKI-SAN...?

ER...
UM...
AH-HEH...
...

HEY, KURTZ...
ONE SECOND YOU'RE GONE, THE NEXT YOU'RE JUMPIN' ME.
HRRGGG
WHAT GIVES?

GAAAAAH!!
SENPAI!

SEN-PAI?!

OH.
UH...

HE'S...

HE'S A DETECTIVE I KNOW.

KURTZ
DETECTIVE

UGAKI
DETECTIVE

VOLUME 2/END

SENSEI! AN INTRUDER!
I SAW AN INTRUDER!
WHAT?!
WHAT'D HE LOOK LIKE?

UMM...
AS BIG AS A BEAR...
UH-HUH...

AND HIS HAIR WAS REALLY... SHAGGY.
もじゃ SHAGGY
もじゃ SHAGGY
...

AND HIS EYES GLINTED LIKE A PREDATOR ON THE HUNT!
DID YOU SEE AN ACTUAL BEAR?!

SATAKE-KUN!

...
KUSA-KABE ...?

UMM ...
I KNOW IT'S A LITTLE LATE...
...BUT WHEN I COLLAPSED A WHILE AGO...
...YOU WERE THE FIRST TO ASK HOW I WAS. THANK YOU!

A-AND...
...YOU WORKED UP THE NERVE TO ASK ME OUT...
...AND I JUST SHOT YOU DOWN. I'M SORRY ABOUT THAT.
SO...

H-HOW ABOUT WE GO OUT SOMEWHERE? YOU KNOW...
...TO KARAOKE...
...OR SOME-THING...

...

HRRRRR

YEAA-AAAH-HHH!!

TURNS OUT IT WASN'T A DATE.
HUH? ARE YOU THE ONLY GUY, SATAKE-KUN?

INTERVIEWS WITH MONSTER GIRLS

Why are they here?!

What does the detective think of demis?

Will Kurtz's secret be revealed?!

Piping hot ramen!

INTERVIEWS WITH MONSTER GIRLS

by Petos

**Volume 3—
on sale
Spring 2017!**

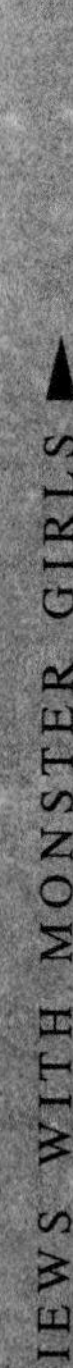

Next time in *Monster Girls*...

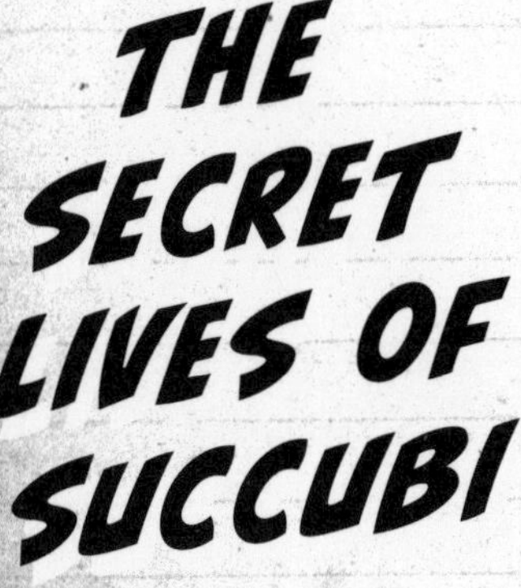

Will we see something more of Sato-sensei?!

INTERVIEWS WITH MONSTER GIRLS

THE FOLLOWING *MONSTER GIRLS*
BONUS CHAPTER APPEARED
SPECIALLY IN YOUNG MAGAZINE.

DING-DONG
キーンコーン
THIS WORLD IS HOME TO "DEMIS"...
PEOPLE WITH SLIGHTLY DIFFERENT TRAITS THAN TYPICAL HUMANS.
THEY ARE FEW AND FAR BETWEEN.
SO IT'S SUPPOSED TO BE VERY UNUSUAL TO MEET ONE.
SCIENCE LAB
TAP
TAP
BUT FOR SOME REASON, SEVERAL ARE AT THIS SCHOOL.
A SNOW WOMAN, A SUCCUBUS, A DULLAHAN...
TAP
TAP
I'VE MET QUITE A FEW, IN FACT.
CLATTER
AND THEN THERE'S...
IT'S SO HOO-OOT!
LET'S COOL THIS PLACE DOWN, SENSEI!
AGAIN?
...THE FIRST ONE WHO TALKED TO ME.

Bonus chapter: Hikari Takanashi, Vampire

HIKARI TAKANASHI.
SHE'S...
...A VAMPIRE.

TAP
TAP
TAP
TAP
STILL NO GOOD WITH NATURAL LIGHT, HUH?
"STILL"? I SWEAR IT'S BEEN GETTING HOTTER EVERY DAY.
IT'S TOUGH, BEING IN THE SUN ALL THE TIME...
WOBBLE

...
TAP
TAP

WHATCHA DOIN', SENSEI?!
YIKES!
POP
YOU'RE WARM! I THOUGHT YOU CAME HERE TO COOL DOWN!

THIS?
I'VE BEEN TALKING TO YOU FOR A WHILE—ABOUT YOUR TRAITS, YOUR FEELINGS.
I'M TRYING TO SUMMARIZE IT ALL.
OOH...

OH! THERE'S ME!
YEAH.
WELL, VAMPIRES.

SUN-LIGHT...
FOOD PREFER-ENCES...
THE NEED TO SUCK BLOOD...
WE CHATTED ABOUT CROSSES AND GARLIC, TOO.
WE'VE COVERED A LOT, ACTUALLY.
PERSONALLY, I FOUND THE ISSUE OF THE CONNECTION BETWEEN BLOOD-SUCKING AND LOVE TO BE ESPECIALLY FASCINATING.
ERK.
L-LOVE...
HUH?
OH, SORRY... I DON'T MEAN TO PUT TOO FINE A POINT ON IT.
...
GUESS IT'S KIND OF AWKWARD, HUH?
...

N-NOT REALLY!
NOT AT ALL!
IN FACT, LET'S TALK ABOUT IT SOME MORE! ASK ME ANYTHING!
HUH?
FWAH

...
REALLY?

OKAY, IF YOU INSIST...
BLOOD-SUCKING APPEARS TO HAVE SEXUAL OVERTONES FOR VAMPIRES...
...BUT HOW STRONG ARE THEY?
HOW... HOW STRONG?

Y-YOU MEAN...
...COMPARED TO A...
...LIKE ...
...A KISS...
...OR SOMETHING?

RIGHT.
LIKE...
...IS IT MORE THAN A KISS?

SEX?!

BUT LESS THAN SEX?

...E...

...

DEPENDS ON THE PERSON...
I THINK.
UM...WELL, OBVIOUSLY...
BUT I WANT TO KNOW HOW *YOU* FEEL.

B-BUT I'VE NEVER BEEN IN LOVE...
I KNOW.
AND I'VE ONLY EVER SUCKED A PERSON'S BLOOD ONCE...
カタ TAP
カタ TAP
カタ TAP
...
NEWS TO ME.
BUT YOU SEE THAT STUFF IN TV SHOWS AND MOVIES, RIGHT?
COM-PARED TO THAT...?
TAP カタ
カタ TAP
カタ TAP
...
HUH?
...
...
...
SHE'S BEET RED.
...
MAYBE I SHOULDN'T HAVE MENTIONED SEX?
OH...
I MEAN...
EVERY-ONE'S DIFFERENT, OF COURSE...

BLOOD-SUCKING WAS TRADITIONALLY A WAY FOR OFTEN-ANEMIC VAMPIRES TO GET THE BLOOD THEY WERE MISSING.
NOW YOU GET BLOOD FROM THE GOVERNMENT, SO THERE'S NO NEED TO ACTUALLY SUCK PEOPLE'S BLOOD!
SO OF COURSE, ITS PERCEIVED VALUE HAS DECREASED!
Y-YEAH, RIGHT!

...
HANG ON.
COULD I BE WRONG TO SEE BLOOD-SUCKING IN MERELY SEXUAL TERMS...?

AS A DISAPPEARING CULTURAL PRACTICE...

...IT MAY HAVE A VALUE BEYOND *SEX.*

MUTTER...

THAT'S TWICE NOW!

HMM...

HRRM...
HERE I'M TRYING SO HARD NOT TO SHOW HOW EMBARRASSED I AM...
BUT THIS IS GETTING TOUGH TO LISTEN TO...

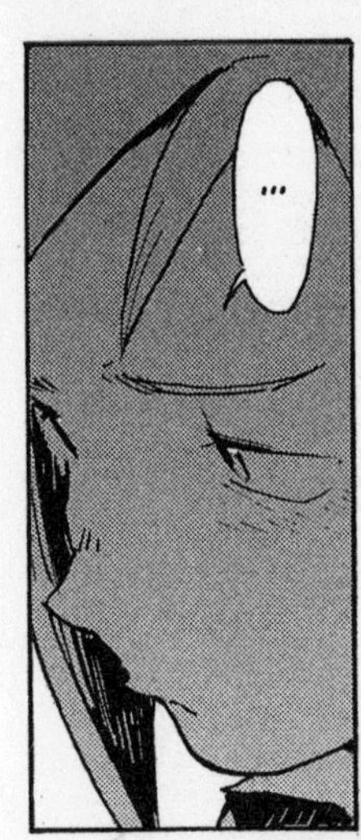
...

!
OH!
ぽん
CLAP
?

C'MERE, C'MERE.

...?

PSST
PSST

ちゅ
PECK

HEE HEE HEE!
GOTCHA! ♡
...
COMPARED TO BLOOD-SUCKING...
...MAYBE A KISS IS...
...A LITTLE EASIER? ♡

かあああ
BLUUUUSH
I SEE!
"COMPARED TO BLOOD-SUCKING, A KISS IS EASIER..."
END QUOTE!
カタ
TAP
カタ
TAP
カタ
TAP
DON'T WRITE THAT!
HAVE SOME DECENCY!

I TOTALLY GAVE SENSEI A KISS!
WHA-AA?!
ON THE CHEEK!

OH, JUST THE CHEEK?
THE LITTLE SISTER

JUST THE CHEEK...
I'M STILL KIND OF JEALOUS.

LUCKY GIRL!!
SAKIE SATO
LIFELONG BACHE-LORETTE

TRANSLATION NOTES

Head jokes, page 56
For those interested in the original Japanese: The memo Kyoko writes is *kubi ga mawaranai*, or literally "can't turn your head" - indicating one is so deep into something (usually debt) they can't turn their head. The joke at the bottom of the page is *kubi wo nagakushite matsu* - to wait with one's neck outstretched, meaning to have great anticipation for something. Thankfully, the English language has many head-related idioms, so our translations can come pretty close!

Foot bath, page 57
A "foot bath" (*ashiyu*) is a basin or fountain full of warm water that passers-by can use to rest their feet. They are especially common in towns with a large concentration of public bath houses.

Niigata Prefecture, page 60
Located roughly in the northwest of Honshu, Japan's main island, Niigata gets plenty of snow and would be a natural place to find stories like this.

Not one of ours, page 107
Many Japanese middle and high schools require students to wear uniforms. The details of the uniform differ from school to school, however, such that it is possible to tell who attends which school based on their outfit.

Kurtz, page 108
The character design of Kurtz is an unmistakable homage to the title character of Shigeru Mizuki's series *GeGeGe no Kitaro*. This series, which began as a manga in 1960 and has been a staple of Japanese pop culture ever since, features a young monster boy and his adventures with the *yokai* (traditional monsters) that still inhabit Japan. The main difference between Kitaro and Kurtz is that Kitaro's hair parts to reveal his right eye, whereas Kurtz's reveals his left.

Young Magazine, page 132
Young Magazine is a sister publication of Young Magazine the 3rd, in which *Interviews with Monster Girls* normally runs.

C'mere, c'mere, page 141
Hikari makes the typical Asian beckoning gesture, with the palm down. To beckon with the palm up, or worse, with a single finger, is considered rude—which is why in anime and manga, characters often do it as an invitation to fight.

Interviews with Monster Girls volume 2 is a work of fiction. Names, characters, places, and incidents are the products of the author's imagination or are used fictitiously. Any resemblance to actual events, locales, or persons, living or dead, is entirely coincidental.

A Kodansha Comics Trade Paperback Original.

Interviews with Monster Girls volume 2 copyright © 2015 Petos
English translation copyright © 2016 Petos

All rights reserved.

Published in the United States by Kodansha Comics, an imprint of Kodansha USA Publishing, LLC, New York.

Publication rights for this English edition arranged through Kodansha Ltd., Tokyo.

First published in Japan in 2015 by Kodansha Ltd., Tokyo, as *Demi-chan wa Kataritai*, volume 2.

ISBN 978-1-63236-387-9

Printed in the United States of America.

www.kodanshacomics.com

9 8 7 6 5 4 3 2 1

Translation: Kevin Steinbach
Lettering: Paige Pumphrey
Additional design work by: Andrea Lesikar
Editing: Lauren Scanlan
Kodansha Comics edition cover design: Phil Balsman

FORTY-SEVEN FEB 1 5 2017

STOP!

You are going the wrong way!

Manga is a completely different type of reading experience.

To start at the BEGINNING, go to the END!

That's right! Authentic manga is read the traditional Japanese way—from right to left, exactly the opposite of how American books are read. It's easy to follow: just go to the other end of the book, and read each page—and each panel—from the right side to the left side, starting at the top right. Now you're experiencing manga as it was meant to be.

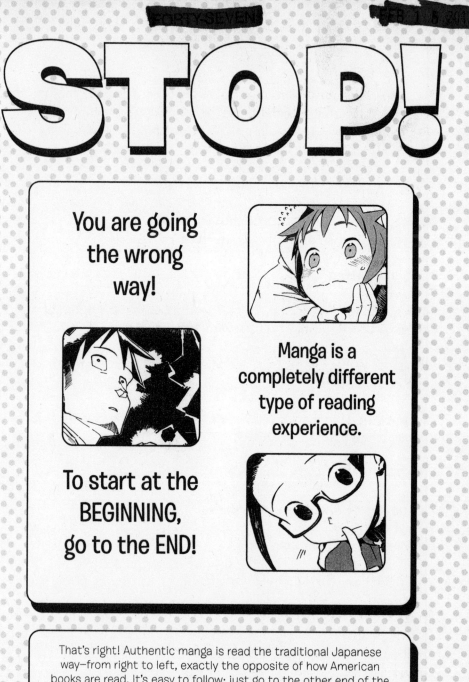